Conve with My *Father*

AS I WALKED THROUGH THE VALLEY

Earthia Jenkins

ISBN 978-1-63630-019-1 (Paperback)
ISBN 978-1-63630-020-7 (Digital)

Scripture quotations not annotated are taken from the New Living Translation of the Bible. Scripture quotations annotated NKJV are taken from the New King James Version of the Bible. Scripture quotations annotated AMP are taken from the Amplified Version of the Bible.

Covenant Books, Inc.
11661 Hwy 707
Murrells Inlet, SC 29576
www.covenantbooks.com

To my best friend, Carmen M. Webb, without whose help and inspiration, I would not have been able to complete this work. Carmen has always been a positive force in my life, an invaluable personal cheerleader. Her efforts were not solely by her voice but in much more tangible ways, including but not limited to her assistance as I pursued my college education, a listening ear as I journeyed through some very dark days, her strength of love and comfort when all around me seemed to have been crumbling, provisions of rest when things became unbearable, and an undying friendship that I will treasure for the rest of my life. To you, my friend, I say thank you, and may God's blessings forever be with you.

To Dr. Gloria S. Simmons, a friend and powerful woman of the Gospel. She has been my inspiration, encourager, promoter, and often my church warden, strongly urging me to complete this work that had been assigned to me. As collaborators in teaching God's Word, I gleaned from her serious and often comedic sharing of teachings, preached messages, counselings, and other experiences she shared to build and shore me up in God's way. She is a visible example of Christ-centered humility albeit filled with power and fortitude. To Gloria will I ever be grateful.

Contents

Purpose

This book was written to share my communications with the Lord while traveling through a difficult valley of time.

I am sharing what I believe to have been letters written by my hands but inspired by God in periods of prayer and meditation during my valley experiences.

I know that as believers, we all have valley experiences, and yet they are not all the same or the same experiential walk. We do not all walk them through the same way. I felt encouraged to share what I consider letters from my Father while in the valley because they helped me so profoundly.

Some of these letters moved me along ever so slightly, while others catapulted me to the next step. Some are powerful words of encouragement while others strong words of rebuke, but whatever the message, they moved me and kept me going.

My prayer is that you find something helpful, or if the writings are not a need for you, then you may share with someone you think may benefit them.

As I prayed before having this work published, God through His Holy Spirit assured me that this work is for

His glory, that His name gets the praise for the results in my life. My prayer is that you are blessed by it for His glory. Be blessed.

Introduction

My journey to greater intimacy and unyielding trust in my Father began when I was forced to make a difficult decision for an early retirement from employment with the United States Postal Service due to illness.

It has been a tumultuous journey, but one that has garnered priceless results.

Having gone through one crisis after another like a boulder traveling down a mountainside in slow motion, I can honestly say thank you to my Father for the journey. I can say this because when I review the journey from ten years earlier, my Father was with me the entire time from the beginning and continuing.

When I retired from the US Postal Service, I had no idea what was ahead of me. The first thing I immediately learned was that my income was not going to meet the needs of my monthly living expenses, not by a long shot.

Although the Lord healed my body from a debilitating condition of fibromyalgia three months after retiring, going back to work the first five years after retirement was not an option because He closed every door of employment opportunity. So for those five years, it was He and I the first five hours of my day. Before any noise from the world or any other human voice, it was He, me, and His Word.

Despite the money issue, these times of communing with Him brought me the peace I needed to journey on.

Many (friends and family) did not understand my journey, but I knew the conversations I was having with my Father to be true and directive, so I followed His direction, although not always willingly.

When I came to a point and needed to hear from Him in a more profound way, He inspired letters to me which resulted in this work that I am now sharing with you. I came to experience "God breathed" which defines how the authors of His Word wrote His messages to the world. He spoke, I wrote, and when He stopped, I put a period to the letter.

There were times I would revisit the writings after some time had passed and knew without a shadow of a doubt that the words came from Him, not my intelligence, not my schooling, not any skill that I may or may think I possessed. They were direct messages from Him to me at a relevant time, and to this day, I give Him glory, honor, and praise for communicating with me in this manner. It was and continues to be effective.

I pray that in sharing these writings of which some or all may be applicable to situations you find yourself in, know that He is a right-now God for real situations, and we all need to be reminded that when we surrendered our lives to Him, we deemed Him to be in charge and must trust His timing for everything.

"Even when I walk through the darkest valley, I will not be afraid, for you are close beside me. Your rod and your staff protect and comfort me" (Psalms 23:4).

Can anything ever separate us from Christ's love? Does it mean He no longer loves us if we have trouble or calamity, or are persecuted, or hungry, or destitute, or in danger, or threatened with death? (As the Scriptures say, "For your sake, we are killed every day, we are being slaughtered like sheep") No, despite all these things, overwhelming victory is ours through Christ, who loved us.

And I am convinced that nothing can ever separate us from God's love. Neither death nor life, neither angels nor demons, neither our fears for today nor our worries about tomorrow-not even the powers of hell can separate us from God's love. No power in the sky above or in the earth below-indeed, nothing in all creation will ever be able to separate us from the love of God that is revealed in Christ Jesus our Lord. (Romans 8:35–39)

I Am Loving You

You are My child, and I am loving you. Not because of anything you have done am I loving you, but because you are My child I am loving you.

When you were yet in your sins I am loving you. As you trust in Me, I am loving you.

In your periodic rebellion, I am loving you.

In your periods of doubt, I am loving you.

In your obedience and disobedience, I am loving you.

In your heartaches, I am loving you.

In your struggles, I am loving you.

In your days of failing health, I am loving you.

In your days of triumph, I am loving you.

In your seeking Me, I am loving you.

You are loved by Me immeasurably.

You are loved by Me untiringly.

You are loved by Me eternally.

My love for you is always active and present.

I am Your Father, and I will always love you.

A Decision

Ownership

I was living within the confines and consequences of unwise decisions made in years far gone. Although my motives for the decisions were pure in heart aimed at helping others, they were unwise, and I operated in zeal without knowledge. The decision was a costly one.

It is God and God alone who must and would release me from this place. It is God and God alone who has caused me to make it through this journey thus far, and I know until its end.

I blame no one but myself. I hold no one else responsible for my conscious and deliberate act. Hindsight and research of God's Word opened my eyes to the error, even though at the time I had such joy in making it happen.

It is God's mercy that this situation will and has been turned to work for my good. It was His mercy alone that this unwise decision did not result in loss of my home. It is God's mercy and forgiveness that lessened the negative impact the decision could have had. It could have been far worse. It is of God's mercy that I have not been consumed with worry and grief. To Him and Him alone, I give praise and glory.

My testimony in detail will help others in more ways than one. As much as one would like to help someone in distress, you should never give or loan more than you can stand to lose. Cosigning debts was an unwise decision that I made that brought me more problems that I could have imagine. It resulted in not only loss money but more importantly loss relationships. It resulted in heartaches that lasted longer than I would have imagined.

Had I not turned to God and began a journey of forgiveness, I would still be bitter today. I could say as David implied, if it was a foe, I could have handled it better, but they were friends, ones whom I prayed for and prayed with. But as stated before, I cannot place blame on anyone other than myself.

Despite the genesis of this journey, God has caused it to work for my good. I became closer to Him. I became more dependent on Him. I consulted Him more in every decision. I sought His face before making decisions.

I experienced Him as a lawyer in the courtroom throughout legal matters that this caused. As I literally sat at the table in court for the foreclosure of my home, God blanketed me with such peace that I had no fear or anxiety and knew He was the attorney by my side. My faith strengthened in knowing He knows and is always there. His hand in mine as I walked brought me comfort. Sometimes He had to pick me up and allow me to wet His neck with my tears when moments seemed unbearable. He reminded me, "I've got you."

My conversations with Him became more consistent and filled with praise. I began to live in relationship with Him that I took for granted. I began to talk to Him more than on my knees. I began to appreciate Him more in everything. I came to know that despite my ignorance, despite my errors even if with good intentions, He will still be there for us and minimize the consequences of our actions. God's love for me is beyond my comprehension.

I have accepted full responsibility and have asked for help when the need was dire. I own this journey and thank God my Father for being here with me every step of the way. I am a better child of God for it.

All the praise and glory is given to my Father who has kept me.

"'For I know the plans I have for you,' says the Lord. 'They are plans for good and not for disaster, to give you a future and a hope. In those days when you pray, I will listen. If you look for me wholeheartedly, you will find me. I will be found by you,' says the Lord" (Jeremiah 29:11–14a).

The Decision

Perspective

We do not always know the path we must take. We do not always know who is to come and go in and out of our lives. We do not always see the trouble and heartaches approaching that must be endured on this journey. However, the one thing we must be assured of is that as a believer, God has gone before us, and He will not allow more to come upon us than we can handle. Come what may, God will lead us down the best path and where challenges lie. He makes a way of escape. He lights our path enough so that we may go through in the direction He has given if we trust Him.

Continuing to seek Him at every turn assures us that we will make it through in His timing, as well as reap benefits as a result of going through. If we seek Him, acknowledge Him in all our ways, He will direct our path. When we stay the course and not allow man nor woman, friend nor foe steer us away from God's direction, we will be successful. Jesus alone is the author and finisher of our lives.

We must keep in mind that whatever life presents us, God is in control. He handles the ups and downs while we walk through them. The operative word is "through." God is in control of promotions' elevated movements, all that pertain to what He has called us to do. After all, it is His call.

We must be strengthened in knowing that He knows all and sees all. Be strengthened in knowing that He wants to be and should be in every decision we make because He knows what is best and when it is best.

Be of good courage and know that who He calls He equips. Be strengthened in knowing that your work is not predicated upon an official document but a willing and obedient heart. Be of good courage as you continue to seek Him for every direction.

He will continue to bless you, to build you, to mature you, and to make you an instrument of His peace.

Sometimes, decisions that we make may appear to be a mistake. This was my experience, and He so graciously comforted me by saying, "Be encouraged to know that this decision in no wise diminishes My calling on your life. This decision is in no wise a failure. Your decision is in no wise a demotion or a denouncement of your call. It is simply a position to take, a path you must walk. Speak and I will be with you. Open your mouth, and I will speak for you. I am with you even now, will be then and will be thereafter. This decision My daughter is one to make as a sign of growth, as a sign of strength, and as a sign of confidence in the One who has called you for such a time as this. Be encouraged."

"Don't worry about anything; instead pray about everything. Tell God what you need and thank Him for all He has done. Then you will experience God's peace, which exceeds anything we can understand. His peace will guard your hearts and minds as you live in Christ Jesus" (Philippians 4:6–7).

Stop and Be Still

A Rebuke

Stop looking for work.

Stop trying to put human effort toward bringing into fruition My miracles!

Stop listening to voices in your head designed to make you feel that *you must do something* in order to bring My work to past. Stop!

Stop thinking that *you must do something!*

Stop believing that *I need help!* It is evident by your behavior and not necessarily by what you say.

My miracles cannot and will not come into being by human effort.

Be steadfast in your belief in miracles because many will come through your hands. Know that My miracles are not made real through human effort. If so, they would not be considered miraculous. *I am a miracle-working God!* Hold on to this belief and watch Me.

Listen, I need you to be still. Stop finding things to do. This is your year of Jubilee wherein I pour into you. It is My time to do. Sit in My classroom, do not move, and let me pour into you. Do not be concerned about your stillness because I am moving in you, even when you are unaware. Rest in Me and be still in Me. Trust in my doing and let Me work.

"So my dear brothers and sisters, be strong and immovable. Always work enthusiastically for the Lord, for you know that nothing you do for the Lord is ever useless" (1 Corinthians 15:58).

Do Not Be Moved

Do not be moved by what is in your immediate space. It is not your permanent surrounding. Do not be moved by anything you may currently see or experience because you may not know it, but I have you in motion. You may not yet see where I am taking you, but you are moving according to My direction for your life.

Do not be dismayed or discouraged by where you are because it too is purposeful. Although it may appear that you are at a standstill, and I am not moving through you, that is so far from the truth. Too often, My children walk by their natural sensory perceptions rather than My spiritual direction. Do not be discouraged because your hands appear not to be busy; you are where I need you to be.

Trust Me and know that I am still in control.

Trust Me and know that I am still at the helm of your life.

Trust Me and know that I am aware of everything about you, your past, your present, your future, your concerns, your ambitions, and the desires of your heart. All there is to know about you, I know. I know your heart, your joys, and your pains.

Trust Me and trust My timing for you. Your heart is filled with expectations that I have already met. You worry about whether I am going to do it or not, but I need you to trust Me to know it's already done.

You are My child. I am your Father. No good thing will I withhold from you because you walk uprightly before Me. You keep Me in mind when making decisions, before you speak, or consider a decision. Rest in Me. Trust in Me and see Me work a work in you that will even inspire you. Stay in My Word. Keep it in your heart, walk in it daily, trust in it as if your life depended upon it. Stay the course.

"He prayed, 'O Lord, God of Israel, there is no God like you in all of heaven and earth. You keep your covenant and show unfailing love to all who walk before you in wholehearted devotion. You have kept your promise to your son David, my father. You made that promise with your own mouth, and with your own hands you have fulfilled it today'" (2 Chronicles 6:14–15).

Hold On!

I am a God who cannot lie. My promises are yea and amen. What you see around you is not your permanency. What you see around you will not remain. The place that you are in and have been has always been temporary. It was never meant to be seen as a place where you will always be, not so says the Lord.

My ways are far above your ways. My thoughts are higher than your thoughts. This is why it is sometimes difficult for you to see My way because your natural eyes get in the way. Your natural view of things causes you to think that is the way it is and will be. Your natural sensing of matters short-circuits My spiritual moves. I am your Father, and no good thing will I withhold from My children who walk upright before me. Those who commit to My precepts and honor My word and walk according to My statutes, I will reward. I will grant you the desires of your heart. I have deposited in you a greatness that you cannot imagine. That greatness in you is for my glory. It is that I may get the praise. The miracles that I have wrought in you, for you, and will do through you is so that others will see the results of Me in you.

Your testimony will infect and affect many lives because they are not typical testimonies. You will be a financial counselor because you have passion and compassion for the downtrodden, because you have been in a place of financial famine and can genuinely empathize and sympathize with the likes, as well as encourage them to hold on because it will not always be that way. I have placed a strong desire in your heart to help with matters others would not extend the same type of help. I have given you the desire to help those who cannot see their way until they have been encouraged to a place where their faith grows, and they believe that with Me, they can do all things. I have given you a strong desire to give to those who cannot give back, a strong desire to undergird ministries and make My work easy for some. You have been empowered to do the miraculous because it is My desire for you to do so. I have placed in you both the desire and My power to accomplish that which pleases Me.

Hold on to your miracle-believing mind. Many have given up on Me performing miracles because they don't think that I perform them in today's times, but you continue to hold out—that's My way. Hold on to what I have promised to you, divine health, wealth in your spirit, wisdom, and the love needed to help those without. You will carry this desire all of your life on earth because it is My desire for you to do so.

This journey has caused you to become a good steward in that which I have given you and are giving you. This journey has caused you to become more frugal and wise in your spending. This journey has changed the way you handle your resources, your money, and for this, I am well pleased.

Your Father

"So be strong and courageous! Do not be afraid and do not panic before them. For the Lord your God will personally go ahead of you. He will neither fail you nor abandon you" (Deuteronomy 31:6).

A Reassurance

Hear Me as I speak these words to reassure you of this journey you take.

I am with you in every minute of your life. I sustain you as you move about your life. I move things out of your way and cause your path to be straight. My eyes are continuously upon you to give you strength and endurance for this time and times to come.

Hear Me on this day that your life is in the direction I have turned it. Your walk is according to My plans for you. Do not stumble because of its direction. Do not be in distress because of your circumstances but walk in knowing that its end is greater than its beginning. Walk in the confidence that your journey is one for building and not tearing down. Your journey is so that you may be a help to others who must endure similar situations.

I am your Father, and no good thing will I withhold from you, but there are times of delay until you are ready to receive. Know that what you see is so small. One day, in hindsight, you will ask yourself, "Why did I worry?" Trust is not an easy lesson to learn, especially when the tenets of the lesson are seemingly in contrast to your present under-standing of living for Me. Some lessons may be difficult to learn but a necessary posture as My child.

Remember, My ways are not your ways, and My thoughts are not your thoughts. So although you do not see or understand what I see and know, you must blindly and wholeheartedly trust that I know what is best. Your trust must cause you to not attend to that which is natural but to the spiritual. Your trust must hold on to the knowl-edge that I am your loving Father who is and will always take care of you.

Review your times past and see that your needs have been provided, i.e. bills paid. Review and see that your bud-get did not meet the need, but it was nonetheless provided. Review every month and see that there were some things you received that you did not request. See that I have met you at every crossroad that you deemed impassable. You can clearly see that I have never forgotten you. I have never forsaken you. I have not allowed you to go without. I have been your sufficiency.

Your trust in My way is the best you can do. Your trust in My control of your life surrenders your hand from try-ing to fix what you cannot fix. Do not try to remedy this journey in any way. I am still in control regardless of how things appear. Do not allow your heart to be affected by what you think people say about you. Do not allow your mind to interfere with My plans for you. Remember, you cannot fix this. Hold on to your thoughts of miracles, your belief and knowledge that I can and will keep you in the midst of trouble. Do not succumb to what things look like or bow down to what things sound like.

Lift your head and walk in the confidence of knowing that I am God, and beside Me, there is no other. Know that I am He who you can run in to and are safe. The world's system is not your answer. I know all and see all. I have gone before you and know your path. All I need from you is your trust and obedience. I've got you.

Your Father

"In his kindness God called you to share in His eternal glory by means of Christ Jesus. So after you have suffered a little while, he will restore, support, and strengthen you, and he will place you on a firm foundation. All power to him forever! Amen" (1 Peter 5:10–11).

Words of Encouragement

This journey is not a journey of grief. It is not to be seen as punishment or something you deserve. This journey is for your up-building to shore you up for greater difficulty, to position you to lead and guide others. It is to help you understand the move of God in the life of believers.

This journey is not to harm you or cause you distress. It is to make you strong in Me. It is to seal you in the way of the wise. It is to send you to places that require immediate knowledge of who I am, knowledge of My Word, and what I can do. This journey is to give you an insight to the wealth and worth of prayer, of peace, of quietness, of stillness, of obedience, of listening, of knowing how to hear, of knowing how I communicate when you are still (act of being still) enough for Me to talk to you. This journey is a good journey. Its yield is priceless. Its harvest will benefit generations after you.

Your journey is a journey to a wealthy place, a place of peace, a place of power, a place of love, a place of confidence, a place of comfort, a place of trust, a place of strength, and a place where you are safe.

You have come to a new place of maturity. You have come to an elevated place of prayer. You have come to a place where My Word is your daily bread. This is a wealthy place. Your place was designed by who I am in you. It was designed by where I have brought you from and where I am taking you. In other words, it is not a one size fit all. Your place is specific to your journey, and it will all work for your good.

Do not allow anyone to make you feel that you are out of place with Me. Do not give weight to opinions that you must have done something wrong in order to be where you are. Do not accept criticism for where you are; they are unfounded. Do not be moved by advice that speaks contrary to the conversations you and I have had. Rely on our relationship. Remember what we have talked about and do not veer from My words to you. I am your Father, and no one knows you better than I do. Unless I am speaking through them to you, it is simply their opinion.

Continue to seek Me as you do. Stay steadfast in My Word as you do. Keep your expectations high. Keep miracles in view. Keep your ears peaked and your eyes looking toward those things and places I have spoken to you about. Know without doubt that I have brought you to a prepared place, a wealthy place, a place where I will get the glory, honor, and praise.

Your Father

Farmers who wait for perfect weather never plant. If they watch every cloud, they never harvest. Just as you cannot understand the path of the wind or the mystery of a tiny baby growing in its mother's womb, so you cannot understand the activity of God, who does all things. Plant your seed in the morning and keep busy all afternoon, for you don't know if profit will come from one activity or another or maybe both. (Ecclesiastes 11:4–6)

A Call for Endurance

This race was not given to the swift nor the battle to the strong, but to him who endures to the end, which shall be saved.

Be mindful of what I have given you. Be mindful of the power within you to speak My promises which are yes and let it be so. Remember how I brought things into being? It was through the power of My spoken Word. This is the same Word that is available to you and the same power that is available to live in you. You, through the power of my Holy Spirit and the power of My Word, may by faith speak things into your life that which is in My Word, those things that are in line with My will.

The power that is within you is a mighty miraculous power that has nothing to do with human effort. This same power raised Jesus from the dead will also bring life to you by your faith. Prayer to Me is your acknowledgment that I am, and that I am the one who reward those who diligently seek Me.

Remember how powerful belief and confession is? It is the same principle, belief in My Word and confession from your mouth which brings it into being.

Seeking Me allows you to acknowledge who truly perform the miracles because it begins with Me. Remember Me and My Word are one. The Word was with God, and the Word was God (John 1:1). So understand that I have already given you the answer in My Word and access to My Word and the power within you to make My Word come forth in your behalf.

Ultimately, it is trust in Me and My Word to do what I have already spoken I will do. I will watch over My Word to perform it and not allow it to return to Me void but accomplish that for which it was sent. It is your faith which activates My Word in your life and the lives you pray for.

Why is it so difficult to see results? It is due to lack of faith that My Word will produce what I say it will produce. It is lack of patience with My timetable to allow the Word to produce what I have destined for it. It is putting one's own will above My will for what you should have or do. It is exalting oneself above measure. It is putting one's focus on the natural before and above spiritual needs that may also thwart the results of My timing in allowing the fruit of My Word to take effect.

Therefore, My child, the answer is to continue to seek Me until the Word is manifested in your life which will surely be My will for it to come to pass. Continue to trust in My Word. Continue to seek My face. Continue to hope for that which you do not see, and in due season if you faint not, you will reap each benefit.

Your Father

"The Sovereign Lord has given me his words of wisdom, so that I know how to comfort the weary. Morning by morning he awakens me and opens my understanding to his will. The Sovereign Lord has spoken to me, and I have listened. I have not rebelled or turned away" (Isaiah 50:4–5).

My Calling

A Prayer of Thanksgiving

Dear Father,

I know that you have called me and anointed me to teach and preach Your Word. You have placed in me the desire to study and rightly divide Your Word of truth not only for my hearing and growth but also for the populace of people whom you have assigned to hear me.

It is to You I give thanks and glory for this privilege. It is You who will open doors of opportunity to bring forth a message You have given to me to bring forth. You and You alone will get the glory and praise for what You do through me. It is not by my power, nor by my might, nor intelligence, nor by human wisdom that this is done, but it is by Your Spirit. It is by the incredible greatness of the power You have given to me.

Lord, I am honored that You chose me and assigned to me gifts of healing, teaching, hospitality, encouragement, and anointing.

Father, I count it a supreme blessing that You trust me to rightly divide Your Word, to handle Your Word with extreme care, knowing that people's lives and well-being are affected by what I say. In addition, my life must reflect the Word I teach and preach. The understanding of the Word begins with me.

Thank You for trusting me to do right with Your Word through the leading and guidance of the Holy Spirit for Your people. Thank You for the creative ways You have given me to teach and disseminate Your Word. Thank You for trusting me to hold Your Word in high esteem as You hold Your Word above all Your name.

Father, it is by Your divine appointment that this is even possible. I seek that what I do with my life and the gifting You have assigned to it will always please You. I pray that I walk in the purpose You have destined for me and always seek direction for every step.

Father, I pray that I never get into self or flesh-directed behavior or power-struck personality or haughtiness or high-mindedness or out of Your direct will. I pray my steps are always ordered by You, and that I operate in the spirit that I may not attend to the will of my flesh.

Father, I pray that I will always allow You to go before me knowing that You will make my paths straight.

Thank You so much for trusting me to do Your will and always want to walk upright before You, trusting You every step of the way. Thank You because I am not anxious about anything because You have instructed me to pray about everything.

Keep my mind, keep my heart, keep my life in the center of Your will. Always place in me both the desire and power to do what gives you pleasure. Let my life be pleasing to You and may I be fruitful in every good work.

In the precious name of Your Son, Jesus, I pray. Amen.

"For God is working in you, giving you the desire and the power to do what pleases him" (Philippians 2:13).

Your Desires Fulfilled

The desires of your heart were known long before they were spoken from your lips or a thought in your mind. Your desires are Mine to grant and for you to enjoy and experience as My child, My daughter whose daily effort is to please Me.

As your Father, I find pleasure in granting the desires of your heart. I find pleasure in the prosperity of My saints, My children, whose daily desire is to make certain that their lives are in line with My Word. Your desires are mine to grant and these I have that My name may be glorified through your testimony.

Your testimony can only be attributed to Me, your Father, because I alone could have brought these desires to past as you have expressed. I alone could have chosen them, open doors that were closed, bring justice from injustice, given you peace in the midst of turmoil, and place love in your heart for those who have not only hurt you but caused you harm. I and I alone could resolve these matters and given you peace while you were in the midst of them.

Your testimony will cause others to believe and hold on to the hope within. Your testimony will lighten hearts that are heavy. It will cause some to take heed to My Word while causing others to trust in what they already know of Me.

Your testimony will restore faith in others who are on the brink of giving up. It will move them away from the edge to a place of safety and comfort. Your voice will cause some to say He too is my God and will do the same for me and more.

Your testimony is My message to many that I have not forgotten despite what their circumstances may look like. Your testimony will allow them to see that the best time is My time, and that I will not allow more to come in their lives than they are able to handle.

Trust these words to know that I, your Father, have sent them, have delivered you to a wealthy place, have healed your body, and restored areas where you had weakened. I have given you the desires of your heart, and your gratefulness is your testimony of Me and to Me.

Your loving Father

"This is what the Lord says: 'I will go before you, and level the mountains. I will smash down gates of bronze and cut through bars of iron. And I will give you treasures hidden in the darkness—secret riches. I will do this so you may know that I am the Lord, the God of Israel, the one who calls you by name'" (Isaiah 45:2–4).

Cast Your Cares on Me

All your worries are My resolutions. All that you present to Me are My desires to fulfill for you. Understand that before you speak them, I know them. There are some that I have given to you as your desire, but they are Mine.

You have gotten to a place in Me where your desires come from Me, but more importantly, you recognize it as such. You have grown to know that what is in your heart was placed there by Me. Your growth and maturity in Me has allowed you to understand the incredible greatness of the power I have placed in you. You understand by praying the prayers you pray, by availing yourself to the people I have placed in your path, by giving you strength for who and what is going on in your life that these are a direct result of My workings.

You have come to a place in Me, where your personal desires take second place to the desires I have placed in you. In other words, your desires are more for the things of Me and for My people. You have matured to a place where materialistic possessions are no longer your heart's desire as much as the things of Me that are far more valuable and far more reaching in scope in terms of what it does and who it touches.

You have entered a wealthy place in Me because you seek more and more of Me not for yourself, but that others may be blessed by Me through you. This is a wealthy place. This is a place I want all My children to be and all the other less things of value will be a byproduct of that which is more important.

Continue to seek Me in all that I am and all that I have for you for Me. Continue to let that which is important to Me be important to you, and you will see the many things I will do through you for My glory. Continue to seek Me and all My righteousness and watch Me perform many miracles through your hands because you still believe in miracles. Continue to daily seek My face and watch the prayers you have been praying fall openly before your face, miracles you have prayed for and miracles you do not yet know about.

These words you write are from Me for your encouragement, for you to know that I hear, have heard, will and have answered. Do not be discouraged because of where you are and how your life now appears to be. I am at work in you in a way that will manifest that it could have only been Me who did such a work.

Be steadfast in your faith in the things I have told you. Revisit them and refresh your memory.

I am God who cannot lie. What I have said I will bring to past. What you have asked have been answered above and beyond your asking.

My child, rest in this journey. Continue to seek Me as I continue to pour out into others that which I have poured into you.

Do not worry about your finances, your bills, all that you owe because what you have asked of Me I have done. What you have sought from Me for years past, I have done. Do not doubt, do not be alarmed, do not second-guess. It all belongs to you. Do not think it is a mistake because it is *not!*

Just know that I have been at work in your behalf for some time, awaiting the right time of maturity for such blessings.

You will now be a good steward. You will now discern who, what, when, where, how, and how much. You will continue to operate in purpose. You will seek Me before making decisions regarding your finances. I am your Father who has done this, and it is marvelous in My sight.

You have continued in the faith during these hard years of lack. You have not left Me when you had little, so here you are with much, and I alone have done this for you.

With love,
Your Father

A Reminder

And all of you, dress yourselves in humility as you relate to one another. For God opposes the proud but gives grace to the humble. So humble yourselves under the mighty power of God and at the right time He will lift you up in honor. Give all your worries and cares to God for He cares about you. Stay alert. Watch out for your great enemy the devil. He prowls around like a roaring lion, looking for someone to devour. Stand firm against him, and be strong in your faith. Remember that your family of believers all over the world is going through the same kind of suffering you are. In His kindness, God called you to share in His eternal glory by means of Christ Jesus. So after you have suffered a little while, He will restore, support, and strengthen you. And He will place you on a strong foundation. All power to Him forever! Amen!

—1 Peter 5:5b–11

But my life is worth nothing to me unless I use it for finishing the work assigned me by the Lord Jesus—the work of telling others the Good News about the wonderful grace of God.

—Acts 20:24

A Reflection

The secret (which is not really a secret) to my growth in Christ is due primarily to our (me and my Father) time together.

More times than not, I do not allow the chatter of the world into my space and spirit for the first five hours after my Father awakens me from a restful sleep.

It is He and I during my early morning walk, during conversations on my knees, during the sipping of coffee on my porch, and/or during the reading and meditation of His Word.

As I become more prolific, steadfast, faithful, and desiring of such communion with Him, the more I want of Him, the more I want to please Him and to do His will.

It is during these times that I have come to know Him better and better. I do not want to trade these hours for no one or no thing. I look forward to our time together, and I sincerely believe He is depositing into me much more than I will ever know because the deposit is not always in concert or in direct proportion with the release.

For this, I give Him all the thanks and praise. It is to Him and to Him alone I have such a grateful heart.

God decided in advance to adopt us into his own family by bringing us to himself through Jesus Christ. This is what he wanted to do, and it gave him great pleasure. So we praise God for the glorious grace he has poured out on us who belong to his dear Son. He is so rich in kindness and grace that he purchased our freedom with the blood of his Son and forgave our sins, he has showered his kindness on us, along with all wisdom and understanding. (Ephesians 1:5–8)

Will You Believe?

Will you believe the things I say to you? Will you accept them as My words, direction, and/or instructions? Will you obey and do? Will you follow the words that I am making plain to you? Will you?

When asking, expect an answer according to My will. When seeking Me, know that I hear you. When knocking, expect an opened door. Let this be your confidence.

I want you to understand that the power I placed in you is operating according to My will even when you don't think it is operating. I am your God, and you are in the throes of the plan, destiny, and purpose I have for your life. Although things may not look like how you think they should look, remind yourself that your thoughts are not My thoughts, and your ways are not My ways. I am your Sovereign Lord who knows all and sees all.

You have walked a far distance with Me, and the enemy of your soul wants you to feel that you are stagnant and going nowhere, but believe in Me and know that I know the path that you have taken, and I am with you at each turn. You seek My face daily, and I know you. Believe Me.

Do not fret about the things you do not understand. Suffice it to say that you are on a road that I have destined you to walk. I am doing a work in you for My kingdom's sake, and it has its timing of revelation and full disclosure. Do not fret about what you see, don't see, or think you should see; these are only human sensory perceptions. My spirit is invisible, but its manifested results are undeniably Me.

Stay alert. Remain grounded. Stay in My face. Keep praying, keep believing, and you will see the results of the work I have been doing in you and through you. Do not trust in your own understanding, your own reasoning, but continue to seek Me, and I will provide you what you need for my daily work in you.

Stop doubting what you know to be true of Me. Stop second-guessing that which I have placed in your heart and mind. Believe and know that I am doing a work in you. I am pouring of Myself into you that you may see what I see, hear what I know, do what I say, and believe.

A Prayer to Believe

Eternal God, my Father,

You and You alone know everything there is to know about me and every situation that surrounds me. It is You I trust above all others. It is You whom I seek for specific direction and instructions for my life. Others can only give their opinion, but You heavenly Father will place me on the right path. So speak, Lord, that I will not only hear, but I will also believe and obey.

Sometimes good is just good and not the best. I seek to believe Your best for My life.

In the name of Your Son, Jesus, the Christ. Amen.

Financial Famine

Remembering
A Prayer of Thankfulness

Father God,

Thank You so much for Your love and care about me although I cannot fully comprehend its depth.

What I do understand, however, is that when I call, You come to my rescue, if not for total resolution in my timing of the matter, for Your encouragement to move me further through.

This financial journey of famine has been a long one, but, Father, You have always given me peace each step of the way. Even when things continued to worsen, my peace never diminished, except for those moments when I took my eyes off of You and threw temper tantrums in wanting full resolution in my timing. You had mercy and brought me back to my spiritual senses.

I have lived in the red for the past number of years, at times, not knowing where my next good meal was to come from or how I would put gas in my car to move about. But, Father, You were always there and never left me alone. Dollar Stores became my go-to sources, i.e. General Dollar, Family Dollar, and Dollar Tree, for all things food.

When my home was up for foreclosure due to mountainous debt, You were with me at the table in the courtroom and acted on my behalf to stop the foreclosure. God, it was You and You alone who knew every minute of this journey and its outcome. I am grateful.

When my home was in dire need of a roof evidenced by water leaks from the bedrooms to the living room, You sent an angel to gift me with a brand-new roof, a French-drain, and gutters. This, Lord, I remember and continue to say thank You.

I want to always remember the things You have told me about my home. Such things that, regardless of how things appeared, it (my home) belonged to me. Despite the financial negativity associated with it, I am not moved by what I see because I know in whom I believe.

You gave me this home not only for the purpose of having a place to lay my head but also for others who may have run into hard times, need a respite, need a place to lay their head, in need of a place of safety, or a place of peace to rejuvenate. You deemed it a place of hospitality and relaxation and prayer. This journey has made me even more certain of this knowing because my situation never prohibited me from meeting all of those needs. They were never aware, nor were they required to fund their stay, stays ranging from thirty days to five years. College students, single moms, those in financial hardships, those from broken relationships all benefitted from your plans. Together, You have always been our sufficiency.

I want to remember, Father, that this battle did not belong to me but to You. I am at peace with knowing that You have everything under control. I choose to remember that You had this all worked out above measure. I did not always see it, but grateful I am able to recall it all.

Thank You, Father, for a miracle of debt cancellation. It will be my testimony for the rest of the years You allow me to live. Every opportunity I receive to sing Your praises or encourage a soul as it pertains to financial famine, I commit to speaking it and speaking it loudly and courageously.

Thank You for the testimony of being my lawyer in the courtroom, for opening doors no man could shut, for making ways where I saw no way, and for the miracles of bills being paid without enough money from the resources I had. If it had not been for you, I am not sure what my life would look like right now because You continue to make a way.

Thank You for Your Holy Spirit who has led me through this process, for speaking directions to me, and for making things clear to me. Thank You for Your wisdom to make sober decisions and become a better steward of that which You have allowed me to manage.

Father God, thank You for Your supernatural manifestation in this area of my life.

In the name of Your Son, Jesus the Christ. Amen.

"Trust in the Lord with all your heart, and lean not on your own understanding; in all your ways acknowledge Him, and He will direct your path" (Proverbs 3:5–6 NKJV).

Trust Me

Trusting in Me should not be difficult. My Word does not change, has not changed, and will not change since written once and for all time settled in heaven. You should, without reservation, trust in it, thereby trusting in Me.

Oftentimes, situations become more difficult or problematic because trust is not consistent but wavering. If your trust in Me is as consistent as breathing or doing anything that comes naturally to you, then you will see an abundance of My work in your life. If trusting in Me becomes as easy as eating food, bathing your body, sitting in a chair, driving a car, or walking a path from point A to point B without a second thought, then you would see more of My wondrous works.

Trust must be a basic tenant of living for Me. Trust must be relied upon. Trust must be a staple, a consistency, and you will see more of who I am. Divine revelations will come more fluidly. You would not have to fast at every prayer juncture to see things come to past but simply trust that it will—that I will.

My people lack due to lack of trust and understanding. They rely on their own reasoning as to how and when I should move. There is no better timing than My timing. I know your end from its beginning and every second in between. Therefore, My timing is the best timing for all that pertains to you. My timing is perfect, flawless. Trust in it (My timing) and trust in Me to know what is best for you.

Remember that My ways are not your ways. My thoughts are not your thoughts. Trusting in that knowing will cause you to see Me and trust Me more. Acknowledge Me in all your ways and trust Me to direct your path.

Live in a way knowing that I have your life in My hands. I will protect it, lead it, and guide it into the way that I want you to go. Trusting in Me gets you to that understanding. Taking matters into your own hands only delay and defer My perfect plans. I know the plans I have for you. I know your expected end. Your trust in Me will get you there in My timing. Lean not to your own understanding because it will take you out of focus and off of Me.

Trust Me for What to Say

The lives I designate for your voice are because you have something to say to them from Me. This is where trust must be expected; that I will give you what to say at the time it is needed.

Trust that when you make yourself available, I am with you. I will speak through you. Your trust in knowing that when you open your mouth, I will speak, will allow the words to flow unobstructed, fluidly.

My call upon your life is for such a purpose: to help those seeking Me, to be available to be used by Me to speak into the lives of those seeking Me, those who have not yet grown to understand Me. Sometimes it is simply your availability and willingness and courage that I need, and I will do the rest. I just need you to trust and know that I will show up. This is true whether it is My Word on paper or through your lips that I will deliver.

My confidence has been deposited in you. Your experiences with Me in recent years has grown this confidence to a different level. Your consistent trust makes it more fluid. You believe that I can speak to you and through you as I did the men and women in My Word, and you are right to believe this because I am the same God now as I was then.

Know that I will use you and anyone who avail themselves for such a purpose. I need vessels of honor so that My work will continue in the earth. Your courage to accept such a responsibility will cause you to be seen as different. Embrace the difference in demonstration of your love for Me, your trust in Me. Trust in knowing that I chose you before the foundation of this world. I wrote your name in the palm of My hand and called you My own.

You are a vessel that I have chosen to be at My disposal for the benefit of others, My Kingdom. I will send many to you, as well as send you to others, your trust in Me as to when and where is necessary. Those I send you to or send your way require your complete trust in Me for the work that is to be done. Your availability and willingness to open your mouth, open your heart, and trust Me to do the rest brings praise and glory to My name.

Your heart is in My hand to protect it. Your heart is precious. It is an extension of Me. Your heart allows you to display My thoughts. I will fill your heart with My thoughts and My will. Follow it when it overflows with My will. It will be clear to you that your direction is from Me. Follow your heart when My words flood it with thankfulness. My words are not grievous but are always for your best. Trust Me.

Trust Me by trusting My word. Fill your mind with it. Follow it, eat it, sleep it, rest in it, and it will always keep you. Remember it does not return to Me void, and I'm always watching over it to perform it.

A Prayer to Trust

Father, thank You for Your faithfulness in responding to my requests each time I ask. You are a faithful God and are concerned about me.

Teach me, Father, how to hear and believe what you say. Teach me how not to dismiss thoughts You send my way but to trust more the Holy Spirit that is working inside of me. Teach me that when my peace leaves a matter, it is for a purpose and for me not to deny your unction from the Holy Spirit. Teach me that when I become troubled about a matter that was once in a peaceful state, there is meaning for a change. Help me to recognize movement through the gently prodding of the Holy Spirit and not to disregard His movements.

Teach me to learn of His tugs when I am going in a wrong direction. Teach me to trust in His messages whether subtle or strongly expressed. Teach me how to lean on Him more and more and for my expectation of Him to be heightened with maturity.

Help me to trust His direction. Thank You, Father.

"Trust in the Lord always, for the Lord is the eternal rock" (Isaiah 26:4).

"The Lord is my strength and shield. My heart trusts in him and I am helped" (Psalm 28:7).

Let your character [your moral essence, your inner nature] be free from the love of money [shun greed—be financially ethical], being content with what you have; for He has said, "I will never [under any circumstances] desert you [nor give you up nor leave you without support, nor will I in any degree leave you helpless], nor will I forsake or let you down or relax my hold on you [assuredly not]! (Hebrews 13:5 AMP)

You Are Not Alone

The love I have for you is beyond your comprehension. Although your flesh, your humanness may cause you to believe that I have left you, that I am nowhere to be found, do not hear you, do not know or care about you or your circumstances, this could not be further from the truth.

I am constantly near you. I know who you are, what you think before you think it, and why you do the things you do. I know your thoughts afar off. I know every desire of your heart, even the ones you are not yet aware of. I know your needs before you ask. I know what you can handle and that which you cannot. I know the things you are ready for, as well as those you need a little more preparation to receive. I am always by your side.

I know your fears, especially those that cause you to place certain criteria on things you have asked of me. I know your worries, family matters, financial concerns, work-related issues, health issues, and concerns about others in your life. I am right here with you, strengthening you as you go. Watching each step so that you will not fall, sometimes picking you up when it's necessary.

I have plans for you that are eminent in its fulfillment. My plans are beyond your grasp, beyond your sight. The enemy of your soul wants you to doubt by causing you to focus on the problem rather than trusting in My solutions that are already stated in My Word. He doesn't want you to remember that greater am I who is in you, and he who is in the world. He wants you to forget that you are more than a conqueror because I have overcome the world, and I am in you and work through you. You are my child, and I will not allow you to feel neglected. My promises are yea and amen. You are never alone.

Fear goes against My Word because I have not given you the spirit of fear but of love, of power, and of a sound mind. Hold on to the truth that you know, the truth that you believe. The truth that is real because it is My truth.

Listen to Me by reading, hearing, and applying My word. I am your Father and know what is best for you, as well as the best timing for you.

Trust Me in the words that I have spoken and continue to speak to you. They are for your guidance, for your protection, for your deliverance, for your comfort, for correction, and all that you need. Let My peace be your barometer. Let My love blanket your soul. Let Me be in you to cause all that I am to fulfill through you. You are never alone.

Rest in My light, in My peace, in My word, and in the understanding of who I am. You are not forgotten, neglected, nor left alone. I am right by your side and will never leave you. I am committed to you.

"I also pray that you will understand the incredible greatness of God's power for us who believe Him. This is the same mighty power that raised Christ from the dead and seated Him in the place of honor at God's right hand in the heavenly realms" (Ephesians 1:19–20).

Recognize My Power

My power is not relegated to four walls or a contained space. My power is mighty, vast, contagious, and powerful.

My power is imparted upon those who have no fear, have no reservation about its effectiveness.

My power is mighty and works in those who seek Me and expect it to produce.

My power has no gender and knows no age. It is the willingness of the recipient to believe and receive. My power produces results. It heals, delivers, sets free, comforts, works miracles, bring things and people into being, and receives no human credit.

My power is miraculous. It is divinely strategic. It causes mountains to move, rivers to overflow their banks, icebergs to melt, fires to consume simply at My voice command.

My power can be instant and immediate. It arranges and rearranges. It extends beyond human comprehension.

If my believers would only believe in its worth, if my children would believe what lies inside of them and its purpose, they would engage my power and cause it to do what it is purposed to do.

There is no greater power on earth than the power that I have divinely imparted into those who believe. Those whom I have empowered to do the work I have assigned to their hands to help build My kingdom.

My power is free for the asking. It costs nothing that has not already been paid. My power is great demonstration of who I am. Anyone who chooses to use such great power must not take ownership as their own but give My name the glory and praise for it being used through them.

My power belongs only to those I have given the right to be called my children. Anything else is false and ineffective. The enemy of My kingdom seeks to mimic such power but fail.

Understand that I say nothing to you that has not already been written in My Word. This is not new. It is simply a reminder of what already exists. My power is your power. Receive it, operate in it, and bring glory and praise to My name. I have given you the authority to use it in the name that is the greatest above all names, and that is the name of Jesus.

Conclusion

My prayer is that you have found something of value within these pages, and that you will be blessed immeasurably as I have been.

We as believers need reminders of the love our Father gives to us daily. Oftentimes, the pressures of life or the journey through a valley experience causes us to lose focus and forget.

There are always reminders that we can pull from if we would simply take the time to look back at all the things He has done for us. We would be reminded of the people, places, and situations from which He delivered us. If we looked back and recalled, we would remember our offences against Him and His Word of which He has forgiven us. If we would, we can remember our unfaithfulness when seemingly everything was right with our world, and we did not need Him for the moment.

When we review in honesty, we will see a Father full of grace, full of mercy, and full of kindness. We will see that He never left our sides in good times or bad times. We would see that He has always been faithful to us. We will remember that when we called Him, He answered and came to our rescue.

This is the Father whom I have come to know more intimately. He is the Father whom I have come to trust more readily. He is the one whom I seek to please in my daily living. He is the Father who comforts and encourages me when times are low. He is the Father whom I now pursue at every juncture, every crossroad because I have come to know more about His constant watch over me to keep me safe.

In my conclusion, I would like to leave this prayer with you. It is a prayer that Paul prayed for the Colossians. I have personalized it as such:

Father, give me complete knowledge of Your will. Give me spiritual wisdom and understanding. Then the way I live will always honor and please You, and my life will produce every kind of good fruit. All the while, I will grow as I learn to know You better and better.

I also pray to be strengthened with all of your glorious power so that I will have all the endurance and patience I need. May I be filled with joy always thanking You, as You have enabled me to share in the inheritance that belongs to Your people who live in the light (Colossians 1:9–12 NLT, paraphrased).

About the Author

Earthia M. Jenkins was born in Beaufort County, South Carolina, but lived in the small town of Port Royal. After completing high school, she moved to New York and lived there for twenty years. She received her undergraduate degree in sociology from Queens College, City University of New York.

She returned to her home state and continued her education and received an MA in Christian counseling.

She is a licensed minister, Sunday school teacher, and mentor. Her mantra and what guides her life is Isaiah 50:4–5 (NLT), "The Sovereign Lord has given me His words of wisdom, so that I may know how to comfort the weary. Morning by morning He awakens me and opens my understanding to His will. The Sovereign Lord has spoken to me and I have listened. I have not rebelled or turned away."

Her daily pleasure is to study and rightly divide the Word of biblical truth and find creative ways of distributing this truth for Christian growth.

CPSIA information can be obtained
at www.ICGtesting.com
Printed in the USA
LVHW082309190321
681669LV00034B/849